31
Day Proverbs
Challenge

She will place a lovely wreath on your head; she will present you with a beautiful crown.
Proverbs 4:9 NLT

Cornerstone Publishing

A Division of Cornerstone Creativity Group LLC
info@thecornerstonepublishers.com
www.thecornerstonepublishers.com

To contact the author or for permission to use any part of this book, please send email to: ebojam@gmail.com

Printed in the United States of America

Proverb 31 Day Challenge
Introduction

Joyful are those who listen to me, watching for me DAILY…Proverbs 8:34 NLT.

Welcome to the RAW 31 Day Proverbs Challenge. This 31-day challenge will definitely be a CHALLENGE. However, you will experience great growth, understanding, and gain wisdom! A pastor once said, "A Proverb a day, will keep the dumb-dumbs away." In this challenge, you will commit to reading a chapter of Proverbs each day for 31 days. You will be challenged to create goals, become more organized, gain knowledge, and become a better, wiser YOU! By the end of day 31, "She (Lady Wisdom) will place a lovely wreath on your head; she will present you with a beautiful crown." Proverbs 4:9 We all have the ability to look like Lady Wisdom! Your crown awaits you!

How the 31 Day Proverb Challenge works.

You will be provided with the resources needed to ensure you have all the tools necessary to be successful for the next 31 days and after.

Each section is broken up by days, one through thirty-one. You will begin reading a chapter a day for the next 31 days. There is a **daily verse** that will be the focus of the day with a short lesson.

As you are reading the daily Proverbs chapter, a space is provided for you to **write down a verse** that grabbed your attention.

Each section ends with a **guided prayer** and a section for you to write down your own prayer.

At the end of each day, take the extra time to assess yourself. Remember, progress is always tracked.

There is also the **Word of the Day (WOD).** These are affirmations you will remind yourself throughout the day. Write the words on your mirror, cut out the WOD, and personalize them.

The **action** steps will challenge you to put the daily Proverbs into practice.

There is a **weekly check-in assessment** to see how your daily habits have accumulated.

Do not forget about the **weekly video lessons**. Try your best to commit to a weekly schedule.

Take the time also to join the private **Facebook group of Real Amazing Women** who are RAW, just like you!

Resources

During this 31 Day Proverb Challenge, we want you to have all the tools needed for success.

Monthly View

The monthly view will help you write out your goals, new habits you would like to develop, and prayer requests that you are believing God for. Plan your next five weeks.

Weekly Planner

A wise person is organized and has a schedule planned. Utilize the seven day-weekly planner each new week. Plan to succeed.

Weekly Goal Check

Each week we will check our goals. A wise person is accountable.

31 Day Habit Tracker

You are provided with a 31-day habit tracker. On the top of your list should be, "31-Day Proverbs Challenge." See how committed you are to gaining wisdom. What other habits can you track?

Project/Idea Planner

God has given you some amazing ideas and projects to dive into. Use this resource to write the plan and vision. Change it often—print additional copies if you must. Get to planning your next amazing project.

Monthly Budget/Payment Tracker

It is wise to have a monthly budget and to understand where your money is being spent. Budget and track your bills. Do not get caught spending without one!

Meal Planner

Having a plan, for breakfast, lunch, and dinner, can help elevate stress. What amazing and healthy meals will you plan?

Day One | Proverbs 1

"Their purpose is to teach people wisdom and discipline, to help them understand the insights of the wise. Their purpose is to teach people to live disciplined and successful lives, to help them do what is right, just, and fair. These proverbs will give insight to the simple, knowledge and discernment to the young." Proverbs 1:2-4 NLT

The goal of Proverbs is to help develop wisdom, discipline, and apply understanding to our everyday problems. By so doing, we will become successful, have sound judgment, and gain clarity.

Word of the Day:

Insightful: I am one who has deep understanding.

Action:

Ask more questions.

WRITE YOUR FAVORITE PROVERB FROM TODAY'S READING.

Prayer

Father, as the spirit of Wisdom is developing in me, I pray for insight and clarity when making decisions. In Jesus' name: Amen.

Day One Self Assessment

1. Have you been struggling with making decisions, or having to make some hard choices? What are they?

2. What would it look like if you made the wrong decisions? What would be the associated risks?

3. What would it look like if you said no?

Day Two | Proverbs 2

"So follow the steps of the good, and stay on the paths of the righteous." Proverbs 2:20 NLT

Finding a mentor is useful for achieving success. If you are planning to go back to school, trying to become more productive as a stay-at-home mom, or starting a new business, having a mentor is good. Seek a person who has achieved success in the area(s) you are striving to accomplish.

Word of the Day:

Student: I am one who studies.

Habits:

Get mentored or follow the steps of those who have achieved your ultimate goal.

WRITE YOUR FAVORITE PROVERB FROM TODAY'S READING.

Prayer

Father, Reveal to me whose steps I should follow as my mentor. Show me one who is God-fearing and loving.

.

Day Two Self Assessment

1. Who could be your mentor?

2. Why this person?

3. Do they live a righteous life?

4. How do you plan to follow their steps?

5. How will their steps help you reach your goals?

Day Three | Proverbs 3

"My child, don't reject the Lord's discipline, and don't be upset when he corrects you. For the Lord corrects those he loves, just as a father corrects a child in whom he delights." Proverbs 3:11-12 NLT

When I was younger, my dad would tell me, "There are three ways of doing something, the right way, the wrong way, and MY way." As a child, I learned quickly that I better do it Daddy's way, because what may have seemed right or wrong did not fit the situation or the current problem we faced. What may seem right, may actually be wrong.

Word of the Day:

Teachable: I am one who is willing to be taught.

Actions:

Become a student.

WRITE YOUR FAVORITE PROVERB FROM TODAY'S READING.

Prayer

Father, instill in me a teachable spirit, one that welcomes correction and feedback.

Day Three Self Assessment

1. Are you okay with constructive criticism?

2. How do you react when people correct you?

Day Four | Proverbs 4

"My child, pay attention to what I say. Listen carefully to my words. Don't lose sight of them. Let them penetrate deep into your heart, for they bring life to those who find them, and healing to their whole body." Proverbs 4:20-22 NLT

Now that you are working on insightful decision-making, you are considering a mentor, and becoming teachable; it is now time to develop the habit of studying. Remember, while gaining insight and knowledge, having good study habits are essential.

Word of the Day:

Attentive: I am one who pays close attention to something.

Actions:

Dedicate five hours this week to study.

WRITE YOUR FAVORITE PROVERB FROM TODAY'S READING.

Prayer

Father, help me develop effective study habits that will become a part of me so that they will never leave.

Day Four Self Assessment

1. What are some things you have learned thus far?

2. Have you purposely studied and reflected on that information?

3. How have you put it into practice?

Day Five | Proverbs 5

"He will die for lack of self-control; he will be lost because of his great foolishness."
Proverbs 5:23 NLT

This chapter is about a young man who walks away from some good stuff in his life to indulge in sinful pleasures. He ends up losing so much more. Your situation may not be as dramatic. You may have stepped away from your weight loss goal, budget planning, business venture, writing a book-for other distractions or pleasures. Instead of eating a salad, you choose a burger. Instead of saving that extra $50, you bought those shoes on sale. Unlike the man who did not rejoice in the wife of his youth, I want you to rejoice in the plans of your youth.

Word of the Day:

Self-controlled: I am one whose emotions and behavior are controlled during stressful and difficult situations.

Actions:

Resist pleasure for 24 hours.

WRITE YOUR FAVORITE PROVERB FROM TODAY'S READING.

Prayer

Father, help me develop self-control in areas that are lacking. Remind me of Your promise of escape as I become more disciplined.

Day Five Self Assessment

1. How have you veered off track?

2. What areas of self-control do you need to work on?

3. Have you discussed this with your mentor?

4. What study habits are you developing to ensure focus?

Day Six | Proverbs 6

"The Lord hates these seven things: eyes that show pride, tongues that tell lies, hands that kill innocent people, hearts that plan evil things to do, feet that run to do evil, witnesses in court who tell lies, and anyone who causes family members to fight." Proverbs 6:16-19 ERV

There is no way one can be an example of Lady Wisdom with the above qualities. This week as we are developing in other areas, let us take a self-assessment of our behavior.

Word of the Day:

Peacemaker: I am one who brings peace.

Actions:

Find an opportunity to build someone up.

WRITE YOUR FAVORITE PROVERB FROM TODAY'S READING.

Prayer

Father, align every area in my life with the characteristics of You.

Day Six Self Assessment

1. Do you carry the spirit of pride? Do others say you are unapproachable?

2. Are you dishonest with others?

3. Are you honest with yourself?

4. Are you a dream killer?

5. When others succeed, does the spirit of jealousy rise up or do you find yourself rolling your eyes?

6. Are you living a life of integrity or gossip?

7. Is your family at peace?

Day Seven | Proverbs 7

"Love wisdom like a sister; make insight a beloved member of your family." Proverbs 7:4 NLT

Proverbs reminds us constantly to love wisdom. This verse says, "like a sister." Ha! I love my sister, but she gets on my nerves! Yet, I will fight till the death for her. Wisdom and insight are like family. It is a relationship that will not be easy to sustain. In fact, it is challenging. If it were not, everyone would be wise. We all know someone who is not.

While applying wisdom to every situation may be difficult, by the end of this 31 Day challenge, it will become easier; wisdom and insight will become your favorite family members.

Word of the Day:

Overcomer: I am one who succeeds in dealing with a problem or difficulty.

Actions:

Give yourself a second chance in the area(s) you failed last week.

WRITE YOUR FAVORITE PROVERB FROM TODAY'S READING.

Prayer

Father, during this time of growth, help me overcome myself and the challenges that may arise.

Day Seven Self Assessment

1. What are some daily challenges you face while obtaining wisdom?

2. What insight did you gain last week?

Congrats! You made it to Week 2!

Check up

1. Did you create a weekly planner, meal plan, project/idea planner, and budget?

2. Did you achieve your weekly goals, budget goals, project/ideal goals?

3. Are you tracking your daily habits? What areas need improvement?

4. What was most difficult about last week?

5. What was most enjoyable?

Day Eight | Proverbs 8

"Common sense and success belong to me. Insight and strength are mine." Proverbs 8:14 NLT

It is commonly known that anything worth having takes insight and hard work. As an example of Lady Wisdom, insight, and strength will come easy when faced with problems or situations.

Word of the Day:

Strong: I am who one is able to withstand great force or pressure.

Actions:

Face your weak areas. Write them down.

WRITE YOUR FAVORITE PROVERB FROM TODAY'S READING.

Prayer:

Father help my sense become common, insightful, and full of strength during challenging times as I reach my goals.

Day Eight Self Assessment

1. What common-sense principles are you applying to reach your goal?

2. Has what you learned during your study time to help you gain insight?

3. How have you been feeling? Weak/strong?

4. Why have you been feeling that way?

Day Nine | Proverbs 9

"Criticize a person who is rude and shows no respect, and you will only get insults. Correct the wicked, and you will only get hurt. Don't correct such people, or they will hate you."
Proverbs 9:7-9 ERV

As we grow in wisdom, we have to understand it is not our job to develop the unwilling. Therefore it is important to exercise wisdom before trying to correct others. For example, do not post on someone's FB comments with contrary remarks or try to correct someone whose lifestyle is not the same as yours. Allow your light, your example, and your love lead others to the truth. Unsolicited criticism or correction will not help you get closer to your goals. It will only become another distraction. Stay in your lane.

Word of the Day:

Growing: I am one who becomes greater and increases over a period of time.

Actions:

Do not engage in unnecessary corrections.

WRITE YOUR FAVORITE PROVERB FROM TODAY'S READING.

Prayer:

Father allow my light to be so bright that it influences others before I even speak.

Day Nine Self Assessment

1. Are you quick to correct others?

2. What can you do to hold quiet?

Day Ten | Proverbs 10

Too much talk leads to sin. Be sensible and keep your mouth shut. Proverbs 10:19

Here we go with our mouth again. Do not allow your reputation, what you are working on, and your relationships to be destroyed because of too much talk. We all know, too much talk leads to gossip. Gossip leads to broken relationships and broken relationships lead to lack of trust. Keep your mouth shut and get on those goals.

Word of the Day:

Uplifting: I am one who makes a person feel more cheerful, positive, or optimistic.

Actions:

Fix what you have broken with your words.

WRITE YOUR FAVORITE PROVERB FROM TODAY'S READING.

Prayer:

Father remind me quickly when I'm about to talk too much or entertain unproductive communication.

Day Ten Self Assessment

1. Do you find yourself wasting time with unproductive talk?

2. Have your words hurt others?

Day Eleven | Proverbs 11

"Upright citizens are good for a city and make it prosper, but the talk of the wicked tears it apart."Proverbs 11:11 NLT

Wise people create solutions. There are many problems in our society, but a wise believer becomes the solution. Is your local park trashed? Gather a team and clean it up. Hungry kids in the community? Feed them. Failing students in schools? Volunteer to tutor. Let us not allow our talk to tear down our community. Be the solution.

Word of the Day:

Servant: I am one who gives their time by performing duties or services for another person or an organization.

Actions:

How will you give back to the community?

WRITE YOUR FAVORITE PROVERB FROM TODAY'S READING.

Prayer:

Father, as a good citizen, show me how my gifts and growing insight will help others and my community.

Day Eleven Self Assessment

1. What areas does your gift help solve a problem?

2. How can your insight lead others?

Day Twelve | Proverbs 12

"The wicked are trapped by their own words, but the godly escape such trouble." Proverbs 12:13 NLT

Wicked words have trapped me. I can still hear the echoes of the hurt from such words as ugly, dumb, and worthless. I believed those words and allowed them to become part of my vocabulary. I would look in the mirror and say, "Ebony, you are so ugly!" I became trapped by words and tried everything possible to not look ugly, to not be worthless, and to not be dumb. I wasted time, money, and self-esteem by trying to undo those words. With every failure, I believed I was the most worthless person. I was going to allow worthlessness to be my death, and trying to become pretty, to break me. It was dumb that I wasted so much time trapped by my words. My actions were not what a wise person would do. As believers, we have the power to escape evil words. The enemy is a liar. The truth is a more powerful weapon. As an example of Lady Wisdom, you are armed with the TRUTH! And the TRUTH will set you free! The TRUTH is, you ARE fearfully and wonderfully made!

Word of the Day:

Free: I am one who is not or no longer confined or imprisoned.

Actions:

Go to a mirror and repeat the last 12 WOD and what you wrote about how Gods sees you.

WRITE YOUR FAVORITE PROVERB FROM TODAY'S READING.

Prayer:

Father help me escape the lies of the enemy and see myself as You see me.

Day Twelve Self Assessment

1. What lies do you believe from the enemy?

2. How do you believe God sees you?

Day Twelve Challenge

Go to the mirror and speak these words over you, as well as what you wrote about how God sees you.

INSIGHTFUL	One who has deep understanding.
STUDENT	One who studies
TEACHABLE	One who is willing to be taught.
ATTENTIVE	One who pays close attention to something
SELF-CONTROLLED	One whose emotions and behavior is controlled during stressful and difficult situations.
PEACEMAKER	One who brings peace.
OVERCOMER	One who succeed in dealing with a problem or difficulty.
STRONG	One who is able to withstand great force or pressure.
GROWING	One who becomes greater and increases over a period of time.
UPLIFTING	One who makes a person feel more cheerful, positive, or optimistic.
SERVANT	One who gives their time to perform duties or services for another person or an organization.
FREE	One who is not or no longer confined or imprisoned.

Day Thirteen | Proverbs 13

"Walk with the wise and become wise; associate with fools and get in trouble."Proverbs 13:20 NLT

I learned the hard way, you become who you hang around. During the time I was walking with "fools," my ways became foolish and hurtful to others. My reputation suffered. To grow in wisdom, achieve your goals, and have a stronger mindset, you may have to make some relationship changes.

Word of the Day:

Genuine: I am one who is truly what they are said to be.

Actions:

- Evaluate your relationship inventory.
- Friends:
- Family:
- Work:
- Social Media:

WRITE YOUR FAVORITE PROVERB FROM TODAY'S READING.

Prayer:

Father, reveal to me the intentions of the relationships I have and remove me from those not aligned with Your will.

Day Thirteen Self Assessment

1. Are our relationships life-giving or life-draining?

2. Do you want to become who you're hanging around?

Day Fourteen | Proverbs 14

"Work brings profit, but mere talk leads to poverty!" Proverbs 14:23 NLT

Let us not talk about what you plan to do. DO IT!

Any of these sound familiar?

"I will lose 10lbs. by the end of the month!" While eating fast food and not working out.

"I have such an amazing business idea!" Yet, never stepping out in faith to accomplish it.

"I will save $1,000 for my emergency fund." While shopping online without a budget plan.

Develop action steps to accomplish your goals.

Step out of your comfort zone and crush your goals!

Word of the Day:

Driven: I am one that has an innate determination or urge to attain a goal.

Actions:

Do one thing that makes you uncomfortable.

WRITE YOUR FAVORITE PROVERB FROM TODAY'S READING.

Prayer:

Father, please help me to continue to work hard towards my goal and take me out of my comfort zone.

Day Fourteen Self Assessment

1. What is your comfort zone?

2. What action steps are you taking to reach your goal?

3. Which steps have been successful?

4. Which steps have not worked?

5. Are your thoughts aligned with that of your mentor?

Congrats you made it to Week 3!

Checkup

1. What are your Week 3 Goals?

2. What was most difficult about Week 2?

3. What did not come as hard?

4. How do you hope to improve?

5. Have you reached your first week savings goal?

6. Have you stuck to your planned schedule?

7. Do not forget to plan for next week.

8. Did you stick to your meal plan?

Day Fifteen | Proverbs 15

"A wise person is hungry for knowledge, while the fool feeds on trash." Proverbs 15:14 NLT

Consider what you are feeding on, mentally, spiritually, and physically. Watch what you eat, what you see, and what you listen to. Trash never leads to success.

Word of the Day:

Intentional: I am one that has an aim or a plan.

Actions:

Limit the amount of trash in your life, from sources such as television, social media, and junk food. Try to avoid them for the next 24 hours.

WRITE YOUR FAVORITE PROVERB FROM TODAY'S READING.

Prayer:

Father, keep my mind off things that do not bring You glory.

Day Fifteen Self Assessment

1. What were you feeding on the most?

2. Did it lead to sin? Stress? Laziness?

Day Sixteen | Proverbs 16

Better to be patient than powerful, better to have self-control than to conquer a city.
Proverbs 16:32 NLT

My husband and I were watching the Kung Fu movie, Ip Man. Whenever someone challenged Master Ip, he won his battles because his opponents underestimated his patience and self-control. Master Ip's opponents on the other hand always lacked self-control. They would rush into battle with him, become caught up in their emotions, and ultimately lose the fight. Do not rush into that battle, or to be number one, or an unproven plan. Your true victory is in the ability to maintain control. Do not risk your business, reputation, or relationship because of power or lack of patience. Embrace the small wins!

Word of the Day:

Victorious: I am one who wins.

Actions:

Celebrate your small wins. Write them down.

WRITE YOUR FAVORITE PROVERB FROM TODAY'S READING.

Prayer:

Father, help me develop patience and self-control that will bring satisfaction and great victory.

Day Sixteen Self Assessment

1. Do you tend to become angry and overpower people during arguments?

2. Are you rushing to meet your goals, rather than trusting the process?

Day Seventeen | Proverbs 17

"Fire tests the purity of silver and gold, but the Lord tests the heart." Proverbs 17:3 NLT

You are on day 17, and I know that you have had some tests along the way. These tests allow us to apply what we have learned. I had some tests come my way as I was writing this book. I had to remember who I am and what I am striving to become. I want to look just like Lady Wisdom. Remember, wisdom, knowledge, and understanding are developed daily. Do not become weary while doing so. Keep going!

Word of the Day:

Encouraged: I am one who is full of hope, determination, and confidence.

Actions:

Write a letter to yourself about how proud you are for completing your goals. Seal it and save it for later.

WRITE YOUR FAVORITE PROVERB FROM TODAY'S READING.

Prayer:

Father, remind me the intentions of Your nature as my will aligns with Yours during any test.

Day Seventeen Self Assessment

1. What grade would you give yourself thus far?

2. What areas do you need to improve?

3. What areas have you grown?

Day Eighteen | Proverbs 18

"A lazy person is as bad as someone who destroys things." Proverbs 18:9 NLT

Rest and laziness are not the same. We have moments of rest, which is a sweet commandment from the Father. Our rest should however not lead us to laziness. Rest allows us to take a break from our work. Laziness is the avoidance of work. I know, laundry sucks, but when it is finished, relief awaits. Keep the end in mind and stay committed to your goals. Commitment is the driving force that will get you closer to your reward. Laziness keeps us away.

Word of the Day:

Committed: I am one who is dedicated and loyal to a cause.

Actions:

Go back through each day to see where you have dropped the ball. Commit to completing those tasks.

WRITE YOUR FAVORITE PROVERB FROM TODAY'S READING.

Prayer:

Father help me stay committed to my plans according to Your will, while exhibiting wisdom, knowledge, and understanding.

Day Eighteen Self Assessment

1. Have you become lazy? Are you just going through the motions?

2. What areas do you need to recommit?

3. Are you using the free tools and resources?

Day Ninteen | Proverbs 19

"People ruin their lives by their own foolishness and then are angry at the Lord." Proverbs 19:3 NLT

Have you heard this before? "Why would God allow this to happen to me? It is all His fault!"

I have been guilty of saying something along those lines.

When things happen, it may be because of our foolish behavior. If we eat healthily, we will have quality of life. If we save money, we will have an emergency fund. It is called accountability. Our foolish behaviors cause fights, poor relationship choices, and ruined reputations. We are responsible for gaining wisdom and applying knowledge and understanding to all circumstances regardless of how good or bad they are. God desires us to prosper and be in good health, now, not later.

Word of the Day:

Accountable: I am one who is responsible for their actions or behavior.

Actions:

During your prayer time thank God for solving a probelm, even if you do not see the solution just yet.

WRITE YOUR FAVORITE PROVERB FROM TODAY'S READING.

Prayer:

Father help me to be aware when I'm about to make a foolish decision and lead me back on the right path.

Day Nineteen Self Assessment

1. What have you blamed God for?

2. How did you contribute to the problem?

Day Twenty | Proverbs 20

"Many will say they are loyal friends, but who can find one who is truly reliable?" Proverbs 20:6 NLT

Friendship is a two-way street. You have already completed your friendship assessment on others. Now it is time to assess yourself. A loyal friend is one who is supportive. A reliable friend is constant and offers a dependable relationship.

Word of the Day:

Reliable: I am one who is constantly dependable.

Actions:

Commit to doing something special for a friend

WRITE YOUR FAVORITE PROVERB FROM TODAY'S READING.

Prayer:

Father, help me to be loyal and reliable. Reveal the areas in which I am not.

Day Twenty Self Assessment

1. Have you been a loyal friend? Rate yourself on a scale of 1-10

2. Have you been a reliable friend? Rate yourself on a scale of 1-10

3. Would your friends agree?

4. How do you plan to improve?

Day Twenty-One | Proverbs 21

"Despite their desires, the lazy will come to ruin, for their hands refuse to work." Proverbs 21:25 NLT

Your desire to lose 50 lbs. will not happen without work. The desire to have more friends will not happen without going out and being friendly. That book will not write itself. Your savings will not grow without sacrifice. Get up and do the work.

Word of the Day:

Passionate: I am one who strongly believes in their cause.

Actions:

Dedicate seven hours or more to your goals this week.

WRITE YOUR FAVORITE PROVERB FROM TODAY'S READING.

Prayer:

Father, provide great passion in me as I reach my goals.

Day Twenty One Self Assessment

1. Rate your work ethics on achieving your goals on a scale of 1-10

2. Which areas need improvement?

3. What affects your passion?

Congrats! You made it to Week 4!

Checkup

1. Week 4 Goals?

2. What was most difficult about Week 2?

3. What did not come as hard?

4. How do you hope to improve?

5. Have you reached your third week saving goal?

6. Have you stuck to your planned schedule?

7. Do not forget to plan for next week.

8. Did you stick to your meal plan?

Day Twenty-Two | Proverbs 22

"Wise people see trouble coming and get out of its way, but fools go straight to it and suffer for it." Proverbs 22:3 ERV

As any driver knows, there are caution and warning signs as we navigate on the roads. God is even more gracious to us than the Department of Transportation because He loves us. God provides warning signs all around and wisdom allows us to see them. If it does not seem right, do not move forward.

Word of the Day:

Foresight: I am one who foresees what is needed or what will happen.

Actions:

Make a list of current warning signs regarding your decisions or plans.

WRITE YOUR FAVORITE PROVERB FROM TODAY'S READING.

Prayer:

Father, thank You for revealing trouble and a plan of escape. Forgive me when I choose to ignore the signs.

Day Twenty Two Self Assessment

1. Have you ignored any warning signs? What were they?

2. What was the reason that you kept going?

3. What consequences did you face?

Day Twenty-Three | Proverbs 23

"Don't wear yourself out trying to get rich. Be wise enough to know when to quit. In the blink of an eye wealth disappears, for it will sprout wings and fly away like an eagle." Proverbs 23:4-5 NLT

We talked much about laziness, yet overworking is just as bad. While hard work is honorable, overworking yourself is dangerous. In the blink of an eye, all you have worked for can be gone. Even worse, in the blink of an eye, you will miss out on making great memories with those you love. Do not forget God's loving commandment to rest.

Word of the Day:

Rested: I am one who is relaxed and refreshed.

Actions:

Start a family or friends tradition. Friday game night, movie night, play outside, etc.

WRITE YOUR FAVORITE PROVERB FROM TODAY'S READING.

Prayer:

Father as wisdom leads me to work towards my goal, remind me to rest.

Day Twenty Three Self Assessment

1. Do you find yourself working long hours? What causes that?

2. What can you do to adjust accordingly?

Day Twenty-Four | Proverbs 24

"Don't be happy when your enemy has troubles. Don't be glad when they fall." Proverbs 24:17 ERV

I had someone tell me they were upset about a failed friendship and no longer being welcomed at that person's wedding. These friends were very close, and the young lady was hurt that she was not going to be a part of such a life-changing event. Out of anger, the young lady said, "I hope their marriage fails, and she has a miserable life!"

I asked the young lady, "How would you benefit from a broken marriage?"

"It will make me feel better," she explained.

Those who strive to look like Lady Wisdom will never look good when someone else has trouble or is hurting. Our goal is to build people up, even those who have hurt us. Never rejoice or be happy when someone, even an enemy, is troubled. I know, it is counter-cultural, but so is Lady Wisdom.

Word of the Day:

Forgiver: I am one who resists resentment or anger.

Action:

Write a list of people you need to let go and forgive.

WRITE YOUR FAVORITE PROVERB FROM TODAY'S READING.

Prayer:

Father help me let go of whatever grudge, hurt, or pain that is associated with that person. I pray only great things for them.

Day Twenty Four Self Assessment

1. Have you secretly hoped that someone would be troubled?

2. How would you benefit if they did?

Day Twenty-Five | Proverbs 25

"To one who listens, valid criticism is like a gold earring or other gold jewelry." Proverbs 25:12 NLT

Constructive criticism leads towards perfection. It is always good to get helpful advice and a second set of eyes on a project or plan. Your plan may need some realistic tweaking. The advice may be hard, but you need to hear it.

Word of the Day:

Flexible: I am one who can adapt to change.

Actions:

Ask someone to review and provide feedback on a project or an idea you are working on.

WRITE YOUR FAVORITE PROVERB FROM TODAY'S READING.

Prayer:

Father help me accept the loving criticism from my mentors, family, and leaders as I continue to grow in wisdom.

Day Twenty Five Self Assessment

1. What kind of feedback would be helpful for you?

2. Have you been in contact with your mentor for feedback?

Day Twenty-Six | Proverbs 26

"Like a dog that returns to its vomit, a fool does the same foolish things again and again."
Proverbs 26:11 ERV

Ouch! Or should I say, "Yuck". I've eaten my fair share of vomit. I have dated the wrong type of guy, over and over again. I have eaten food that I know is not good for me, repeatedly. I have made the same mistakes, over and over, and OVER again.

During these last 26 days, have you found yourself eating leftover vomit? Have you fully committed to your goals, or have you fallen back to the same destructive cycle? Have you gotten off track with your budget plans? Are you still making excuses as to why you cannot step out in faith and start that business? Are you still eating your feelings, becoming easily upset, holding grudges? How does that old vomit taste?

Word of the Day:

Perfected: I am one who has all that is required.

Actions:

Find areas in which you are struggling that need perfecting.

WRITE YOUR FAVORITE PROVERB FROM TODAY'S READING.

Prayer:

Father perfect me in all of Your ways and forgive me when I return to my vomit.

Day Twenty Six Self Assessment

1. What is your choice of vomit? (example: Dating the wrong guy? Eating the wrong foods? Making excuses?)

2. Have you confessed this to your mentor?

Day Twenty-Seven | Proverbs 27

"**Don't brag about tomorrow, since you don't know what the day will bring.**" Proverbs 27:1 NLT

Planning for tomorrow is important. Bragging about it can lead to embarrassment. I see you working hard on your goals and I stand in agreement with you as you are starting to look like Lady Wisdom. You are a goal crusher. While doing so, you do not have to broadcast what you plan to do. Work in silence and allow your achievements speak for themselves.

Word of the Day:

Inspiring: I am one who leads others to greater levels.

Actions:

Journal your achievements past and present

WRITE YOUR FAVORITE PROVERB FROM TODAY'S READING.

Prayer:

Father help me to maintain a humble and quiet nature while working on my goals.

Day Twenty Seven Self Assessment

1. How do you address the spirit of pride when it rises up?

2. What achievements are you proud of?

.

Day Twenty-Eight | Proverbs 28

"Whoever hides their sins will not be successful, but whoever confesses their sins and stops doing wrong will receive mercy." Proverbs 28:13 ERV

Sin will always come to light. Church leaders have been caught in scandals. CEOs and major executives have been involved in unfair deals. Greed, sex, and lies have motivated unrighteous behaviors. Those involved risked their reputation, career, and freedom for moments of pleasure or monetary gain. If there are any issues of sin you are dealing with, resolve it now. Confess your sins to your church leader or mentor. Remaining righteous and being full of love will bestow upon you, honor and success.

Word of the Day:

Purity: I am one who is virtuous in all her ways.

Actions:

Find a safe person to confess your sins to.

WRITE YOUR FAVORITE PROVERB FROM TODAY'S READING.

Prayer:

Father, please forgive me of my sins. As a lady of wisdom, help all my actions be pure and honourable.

Day Twenty Eight Self Assessment

1. What area of sin are you struggling with?

2. What would it look like if your sins were revealed?

3. What steps are you taking to overcoming your sin?

Congrats you made it to week 5!

Checkup

1. Week 5 Goals?

2. What was most difficult about Week 4?

3. What did not come as hard?

4. How do you hope to improve?

5. Have you reached your third week saving goal?

6. Have you stuck to your planned schedule?

7. Do not forget to plan for next week.

8. Did you stick to your meal plan?

Day Twenty-Nine | Proverbs 29

"Fearing people is a dangerous trap, but trusting the Lord means safety." Proverbs 29:25 NLT

You have made it this far, and we have not addressed fear. You have developed wisdom, knowledge, understanding, and established a plan or goal to step out in faith. Maybe you are ready to launch that book, share your weight loss tips with others, or even reach out to that person to mend a broken relationship. But what if they say, "NO?" "No," to publishing your book. "No," to hearing about another weight loss program, or "no" to repairing that broken relationship. Does that create fear in you?

Test it out.

"NO!"

Did anything happen?

Did you lose anything that you did not have before?

Of course you did not.

Fear is a lie! As my pastor says, fear is the false representation of what is real.

Get to as many "no's" so you can gain your yeses! Doors will open, and relationships will be won and repaired.

Remember, God's provision is great!

Word of the Day:

Fearless: I am one who is courageous.

Actions:

Commit to embracing NO. Make a list of people you can ask, seek, and find!

WRITE YOUR FAVORITE PROVERB FROM TODAY'S READING.

Prayer:

Father grant me bravery and peace even when others tell me no.

Day Twenty Nine Self Assessment

1. Did you call, ask, seek, and find? How did it go?

2. How many yeses did you receive?

Day Thirty | Proverbs 30

"Ants—they aren't strong, but they store up food all summer." Proverbs 30:25 NLT

Budget and save. Budget and save. Budget and save! We have always lived in uncertain times, but more so now than ever before. Many of us are now realizing the importance of saving. There are many free resources to help you budget and save. Gain knowledge, wisdom, and understanding of a practical budget. Remember, Lady Wisdom is never broke.

Word of the Day:

Mindful: I am one who is sensible in her dealings.

Actions:

Create your budget and start your emergency fund.

WRITE YOUR FAVORITE PROVERB FROM TODAY'S READING.

Prayer:

Father you are my provision, and I trust in You. Remind me when I overspend and how to save.

Day Thirty Self Assessment

1. How are your savings and budgeting going?

2. Did you reach your financial goal?

Day Thirty-One | Proverbs 31

"When she speaks, her words are wise, and she gives instructions with kindness. She carefully watches everything in her household and suffers nothing from laziness." Proverbs 31:26-27 NLT

You are LADY WISDOM. Have you noticed that you speak differently, your words are wiser, and you are full of kindness? You have carefully saved for emergencies and crushed some major goals! You lack nothing because you are more productive. You gain honor because you know what to say and how to say it. You are more at peace because Lady Wisdom is who you reflect.

Word of the Day:

Rewarded: I am one who is acknowledged for accomplishing goals.

Actions:

Read that letter you wrote to yourself! How do you plan to celebrate?

WRITE YOUR FAVORITE PROVERB FROM TODAY'S READING.

Prayer:

Father thank You for bringing me through this wisdom training. I will continue to commit to living a Godly life filled with wisdom.

Day Thirty One Self Assessment

1. What was most challenging about this study?

2. How have you changed?

Resources

Monthly View

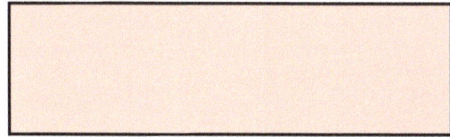

Top 3

- _____
- _____
- _____

Other Goals

- _____
- _____
- _____
- _____
- _____
- _____
- _____
- _____
- _____
- _____

Notes

M	T	W	T	F	S	S

Prayer Request

- / _____
- / _____
- / _____
- / _____
- / _____
- / _____

Week OF

	MONDAY	TUESDAY	WEDNESDAY	THURSDAY	FRIDAY	WEEKEND
6:00						
7:00						
8:00						
9:00						
10:00						
11:00						
12:00						
1:00						
2:00						
3:00						
4:00						
5:00						
6:00						
7:00						
8:00						
9:00						
10:00						
11:00						

Weekly Goals Check

Week One   Week Two   Week Three   Week Four   Week Five

GOAL:

Deadline   Date Achieved

IMPORTANT STEPS:

○ _____

○ _____

○ _____

○ _____

○ _____

○ _____

DOODLE IDEAS:

She will present you with a beautiful crown. Proverbs 4:9

Habit Tracker

	JAN	FEB	MAR	APR	MAY	JUN
	JUL	AUG	SEP	OCT	NOV	DEC

	1	2	3	4	5	6	7	8	9	10	11	12	13	14	15	16	17	18	19	20	21	22	23	24	25	26	27	28	29	30	31
AM Prayer time	■	■	■	■	■	■	■	■		■	■																				
HomeSchool								■				■	■	■	■	■															
Master Study	■	■	■	■			■	■																							

Habit Tracker

JAN FEB MAR APR MAY JUN
JUL AUG SEP OCT NOV DEC

	1	2	3	4	5	6	7	8	9	10	11	12	13	14	15	16	17	18	19	20	21	22	23	24	25	26	27	28	29	30	31

Project/Idea PLANNER

Name:

Start Date: Complete Date:

Specifics:	Sket It Out:

To Do:

- ○ _____
- ○ _____
- ○ _____
- ○ _____
- ○ _____
- ○ _____
- ○ _____
- ○ _____
- ○ _____
- ○ _____
- ○ _____
- ○ _____
- ○ _____
- ○ _____

Investment

Monthly BUDGET

Income	EXPECTED	ACTUAL	DIFFERENCE
Bills and Giving			
Personal			

Payment TRACKER

BILL	DUE	$	J F M A M J J A S O N D
			○○○○○○○○○○○○
			○○○○○○○○○○○○
			○○○○○○○○○○○○
			○○○○○○○○○○○○
			○○○○○○○○○○○○
			○○○○○○○○○○○○
			○○○○○○○○○○○○
			○○○○○○○○○○○○
			○○○○○○○○○○○○
			○○○○○○○○○○○○
			○○○○○○○○○○○○
			○○○○○○○○○○○○
			○○○○○○○○○○○○
			○○○○○○○○○○○○
			○○○○○○○○○○○○
			○○○○○○○○○○○○
			○○○○○○○○○○○○
			○○○○○○○○○○○○
			○○○○○○○○○○○○
			○○○○○○○○○○○○
			○○○○○○○○○○○○

Meal PLANNER

MONDAY
- *B*
- *L*
- *D*

TUESDAY
- *B*
- *L*
- *D*

WEDNESDAY
- *B*
- *L*
- *D*

THURSDAY
- *B*
- *L*
- *D*

FRIDAY
- *B*
- *L*
- *D*

SATURDAY
- *B*
- *L*
- *D*

SUNDAY
- *B*
- *L*
- *D*

PRODUCE
○
○
○
○
○
○
○
○
○

MEATS
○
○
○
○
○
○
○
○
○

CANNED
○
○
○
○
○
○
○
○
○

FROZEN
○
○
○

Notes

Notes

Notes

Notes

Notes

Notes

Notes

Notes

Notes

www.ingramcontent.com/pod-product-compliance
Lightning Source LLC
Chambersburg PA
CBHW041429090426
42744CB00002B/10